Delicious Ways to Pickle Eggs

Simple Recipes for Preserving Hard-Boiled Eggs

BY

Stephanie Sharp

Thank you so much for purchasing my book! As a reward for your purchase, you can now receive free books sent to you every day. All you have to do is just subscribe to the list by entering your email address in the box below and I will send you a notification every time I have a free promotion running. The books will absolutely be free with no work at all from you!

Who doesn't want free books? No one! There are free and discounted books every day, and an email is sent to you 1-2 days beforehand to remind you so you don't miss out. It's that easy!

Just visit the link or scan QR-code to get started!

https://stephanie-sharp.subscribemenow.com

Table of Contents

Introduction

Are you looking for new and delicious pickled egg recipes? Do you want a unique appetizer to serve at your next big gathering? Then give one of these amazing pickled egg recipes a try when you want a tasty treat to serve with some crackers, cheese or as a protein-packed snack.

These methods are simple to follow and contain ingredients found in any grocery store or farmers' market. Read on for more useful information on how to boil and peel and egg and the best way to get the most flavor from your pickling method.

Chipotle and Adobo Pickled Eggs

The sauce from the chipotle peppers is spicy and delicious when used in this pickling recipe. I like to slice these tasty treats up and serve with some sauce on the side.

Preparation Time: 10 minutes

Servings: 12

Ingredients:

- 16 ounces distilled white vinegar
- 16 ounces water
- 2 crushed garlic cloves
- 1 quartered onion
- ½ ounce salt
- 1 ounce white sugar
- 2 canned chipotle chilies
- ½ ounce adobo sauce from canned chipotle peppers
- 12 peeled hard-boiled eggs

Directions:

1. Place all ingredients in a large pot except for eggs and bring mixture to a boil.

2. Cook for 15 minutes until onion is translucent.

3. Arrange hard-boiled eggs in clean pickling jars. Pour boiling brine through a fine mesh sieve into the jars to cover eggs. Cover jars and chill for 3-4 days.

Balsamic Eggs

The intoxicating scent of balsamic vinegar always makes my mouth water. This recipe is best when served with some balsamic drizzled over the eggs before serving.

Preparation Time:15 minutes

Servings:24

Ingredients:

- 24 peeled hard-boiled eggs
- 2 sliced onions
- 16 ounces balsamic vinegar
- 32 ounces water
- 2 ounces white sugar
- 35 peppercorns
- 20 garlic cloves, mashed into a paste
- 4 ounces beet juice
- 6 green cayenne chiles, cut in half along the length
- 6 red cayenne chiles, cut in half along the length

Directions:

2. Place hard-boiled eggs in a large glass jar.

3. Mix the rest of the ingredients in a pot and bring to a boil. Remove from heat immediately and let mixture cool to room temperature.

4. Pour brine into the jar with the eggs and seal tightly. Chill for 4-5 days before serving.

Deviled Pickled Eggs

The creamy filling of these deviled eggs tastes amazing with some paprika sprinkled over. I like to make these for office potlucks or family barbecues.

Preparation Time: 20 minutes

Servings: 12

Ingredients:

- 16 ounces canned sliced beets, drained with liquid reserved
- 8 ounces white sugar
- 6 ounces distilled white vinegar
- 10 whole cloves
- ¼ ounce salt
- 1/4 teaspoon ground black pepper
- 2 bay leaves
- 12 peeled hard-boiled eggs
- 2 ounces mayonnaise
- 1 teaspoon sweet pickle relish
- 1 teaspoon prepared yellow mustard

Directions:

1. Mix 8 ounces of reserved beet juice with white sugar, white vinegar, cloves, salt, pepper and bay leaves in a large saucepan and bring to a boil.

2. Reduce heat and simmer mixture for 5 minutes until sugar dissolves.

3. Combine beets and hard-boiled eggs in a large bowl and pour hot brine over. Chill for 3-4 days.

4. Drain beets and eggs and discard brine.

5. Cut each egg in half along the length and scoop out yolks into a bowl. Mix yolks with mayonnaise, mustard and relish until smooth.

6. Spoon yolk mixture into each hollowed-out egg and serve with beets on a serving dish.

Egg Farmer Pickled Eggs

Use the freshest farm eggs for this amazing pickled egg recipe. I like to serve these with some mustard on the side.

Preparation Time: 12 minutes

Servings: 12

Ingredients:

- 16 ounces white vinegar
- 8 ounces water
- 1 teaspoon salt
- 1 ounce fresh ginger root, sliced
- 1 teaspoon black peppercorns
- 1 teaspoon mustard seed
- 1 bay leaf
- 12 peeled hard-boiled eggs

Directions:

1. Combine all the ingredients except for eggs in a saucepan on medium heat and bring to a boil. Reduce the heat and simmer for 5 minutes.

2. Remove pan from heat and bring to room temperature.

3. Transfer hard-boiled eggs to a jar with a lid and pour vinegar mixture over the eggs until they are covered. Seal the jar and chill for 2-3 days before serving.

Amazing Pickled Eggs

The eggs taste delicious after spending 1-2 weeks soaking up the delicious brine in this recipe. I love the colour of the eggs after marinating.

Preparation Time: 10 minutes

Servings: 12

Ingredients:

- 8 ounces of beet juice from a can of pickled beets
- 8 ounces white vinegar
- 20 ounces water
- 4 ounces red wine
- 1 chopped clove garlic
- 1 teaspoon pickling spice
- 1 bay leaf
- 1/2 teaspoon salt
- 12 peeled hard-boiled eggs
- 1 chopped onion

Directions:

1. Combine beet juice, water, vinegar and wine in a large glass jar. Stir in garlic, bay leaf, spices and salt until well mixed. Add eggs and onion and seal the jar. Chill for 7-10 days before serving.

Pickled Eggs II

These spicy pickled eggs are delicious when served with some crackers and cheese. The flavor of the brine is more intense the longer the eggs sit.

Preparation Time: 10minutes

Servings: 8

Ingredients:

- 12 ounce jar hot yellow peppers with brine
- 12 ounces water
- 8 ounces white wine vinegar
- 1 ounce pickling spice
- ½ ounce white sugar
- 1/3 ounce salt
- 1 teaspoon turmeric, ground
- 8 peeled hard-boiled eggs

Directions:

Stir all ingredients together except for eggs in a 64-ounce mason jar. Add eggs to the brine and seal the jar. Chill for 2-4 days before serving.

Quick Pickled Eggs with Beets

If you don't have a week to wait for pickled eggs then give this recipe a try. After 2 days of marinating, you will have a delicious treat to eat with friends and family.

Preparation Time: 10minutes

Servings: 8

Ingredients:

- 8 peeled hard-boiled eggs
- 15 ounces canned sliced beets, liquid reserved
- 4 ounces white vinegar
- 4 ounces white sugar
- 4 ounces water
- 1/2 teaspoon cinnamon, ground

Directions:

1. Place peeled eggs in a glass jar with a lid.

2. Combine the rest of the ingredients in saucepan and bring to a boil. Stir until sugar dissolves. Pour mixture over the eggs in the jar and seal the container. Chill for 1-2 days before serving.

Mustard Pickled Eggs

Apple cider vinegar has many dietary functions, but my favourite would be using it in this pickled egg recipe. The taste is explosive especially when served on some toast.

Preparation Time:5 minutes

Servings:6

Ingredients:

- 6 peeled hard-boiled eggs
- 1/2 teaspoon mustard powder
- ¼ ounce cornstarch
- 1 teaspoon white sugar
- 1/2 teaspoon turmeric, ground
- 1 teaspoon salt
- 16 ounces apple cider vinegar

Directions:

Place eggs in a 32-ounce jar.

Combine mustard, cornstarch, sugar, salt and turmeric in a pan and add enough vinegar to make a paste with the mixture. Add the rest of the vinegar and bring to a boil. Stir often.

Pour the mixture over the eggs in the jar and seal container with a lid. Chill for 3-4 days before serving.

Yellow Pickled Peppers

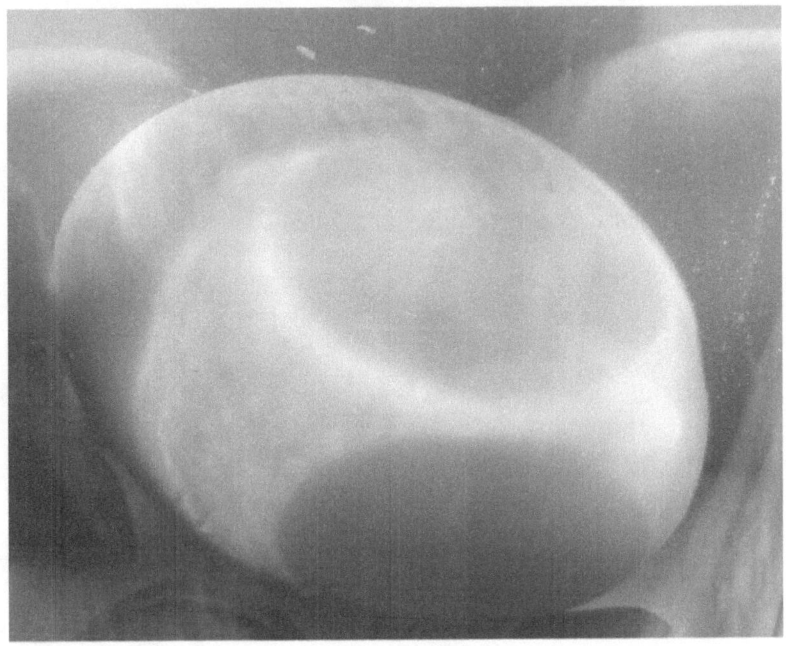

You will fall in love when you take your first bite of these spicy treats. I like to slice them up and serve them with some crackers.

Preparation Time: 15 minutes

Servings: 12

Ingredients:

- 12 peeled hard-boiled eggs
- 1 medium thinly sliced onion
- 6 ounces water
- 8 ounces white sugar
- 10 ounces white vinegar
- 1/3 ounce salt
- 1/4 teaspoon garlic powder
- 1 teaspoon dried dill weed
- 1/2 teaspoon mustard seed

Directions:

1. Put hard-boiled eggs in a large glass jar.

2. Mix all ingredients in a large pan and bring to a boil. Reduce heat and simmer on low for 5-7 minutes.

3. Pour hot liquid over the eggs in the jar and seal. Chill for 4-5 days in the refrigerator and serve.

Pickled Red Beets Eggs

This recipe is another one that uses red beets in the brine. The lovely red colour looks very pretty when served surrounded by green vegetables and crackers.

Preparation Time:25 minutes

Servings:12

Ingredients:

- 15 ounce can beets, liquid reserved
- 1 thinly sliced onion
- 12 peeled hard-boiled eggs
- 2 ounces white sugar
- 4 ounces vinegar

Directions:

1. Pour liquid from can of beets into a pan. Combine beets, onion and eggs in a large glass jar with a lid.

2. Add sugar and vinegar to the beet liquid in the pan and bring to a boil. Reduce heat to low and simmer for 15 minutes.

3. Pour juice mixture from the pan into the jar with the eggs and seal. Chill in the refrigerator for 3-4 days.

Quick And Easy Pickled Eggs

In less than a week you will have delicious and savoury eggs that make the perfect snack. You can also scoop out the yolk and mix it with some mayonnaise for egg salad or filling for deviled eggs.

Preparation Time:25 minutes

Servings:12

Ingredients:

- 12 peeled hard-boiled eggs
- 8 ounces white vinegar
- 4 ounces water
- 1 ounce coarse salt
- 1 ounce pickling spice
- 1 sliced onion
- 5 black peppercorns

Directions:

1. Put eggs in a 32-ounce lidded jar with a wide mouth.

2. Combine the rest of the ingredients in a saucepan except for 2-3 slices of onion and bring to a boil. Pour mixture over the eggs in jar. Top eggs with the reserved slices of onion and seal.

3. Cool mixture to room temperature and chill in the refrigerator for 3-4 days.

Pickled Eggs III

This simple recipe is a quick method for pickling eggs that tastes amazing. The longer you let these eggs sit, the more intense the flavor will be.

Preparation Time:25 minutes

Servings:12

Ingredients:

- 12 peeled hard-boiled extra-large eggs
- 12 ounces distilled white vinegar
- 12 ounces water
- ½ ounce pickling spice
- 1 crushed garlic clove
- 1 bay leaf

Directions:

1. Mix vinegar, water and pickling spice in a pan on medium heat and bring to a boil. Mix in garlic and bay leaf. Remove pan from heat.

2. Place eggs in a large glass container with a lid and cover with the hot liquid from the pan. Seal and refrigerate for 8-10 days before serving.

Garlic Pickled Eggs

I like to make these pickled eggs for large gatherings and serve them with some mayonnaise and an ice-cold beer. This recipe also makes excellent egg salad for sandwiches.

Preparation Time: 20 minutes

Servings: 12

Ingredients:

- 12 peeled hard-boiled eggs
- 1 sliced onion, cut into rings
- 8 ounces distilled white vinegar
- 8 ounces water
- 2 ounces white sugar
- 10 peeled cloves garlic

Directions:

1. Put hard-boiled eggs and onion in a 32-ounce jar with a lid.

2. Place the rest of the ingredients in a medium pan and bring to a boil. Remove pan from heat and let sit for 15-20 minutes.

3. Pour mixture into the jar with the eggs and seal. Refrigerate for 7-10 days before serving.

Pickled Eggs IV

The cinnamon in this recipe adds a lovely spicy flavor to these eggs you will love. I like to serve these eggs at family picnics with some mayonnaise and crackers.

Preparation Time:10 minutes

Servings:6

Ingredients:

- 15 ounce can red beets, juice reserved
- 2 ounces brown sugar
- 4 ounces white vinegar
- 4 ounces cold water
- 1 small cinnamon stick
- 4 whole cloves
- 1/2 teaspoon salt
- 6 peeled hard-boiled eggs

Directions:

1. Pour juice from the canned beets into a medium saucepan. Add the rest of the ingredients except for the beets and eggs to the juice and cook for 8 minutes on medium heat. Stir occasionally.

2. Add beets to the mixture in the pan and cook for another 2 minutes until heated through.

3. Place eggs in a large mason jar with a lid. Pour hot mixture from the pan into the jar and seal. Chill for 5-7 days in the refrigerator.

Sweet Pickled Eggs

If you are a fan of sweet pickles then you will love this recipe. Slice these eggs up and serve them with some cheese, crackers and slices of cucumber as a treat.

Preparation Time: 10 minutes

Servings: 12

Ingredients:

- 12 peeled hard-boiled eggs
- 1 large sliced onion, cut into rings
- 16 ounces white wine vinegar
- 16 ounces water
- 1 teaspoon salt
- 4 ounces white sugar
- ½ ounce pickling spice, wrapped in cheesecloth

Directions:

1. Combine wine vinegar, water, salt and sugar in a pan on medium heat and cook for 5 minutes until sugar dissolves.

2. Arrange one layer of eggs followed by onion in large glass jar with a lid and continue this layering until the eggs and onions are all used, leaving 1" of space at the top.

3. Add spice in the cheesecloth to the mixture in the pan and swirl it around for 45 seconds. Remove cheesecloth and pour mixture from the pan into the jar with the eggs. Leave ¼" space at the top.

4. Seal with a lid and chill for 7-14 days before serving.

Sriracha Pickled Eggs

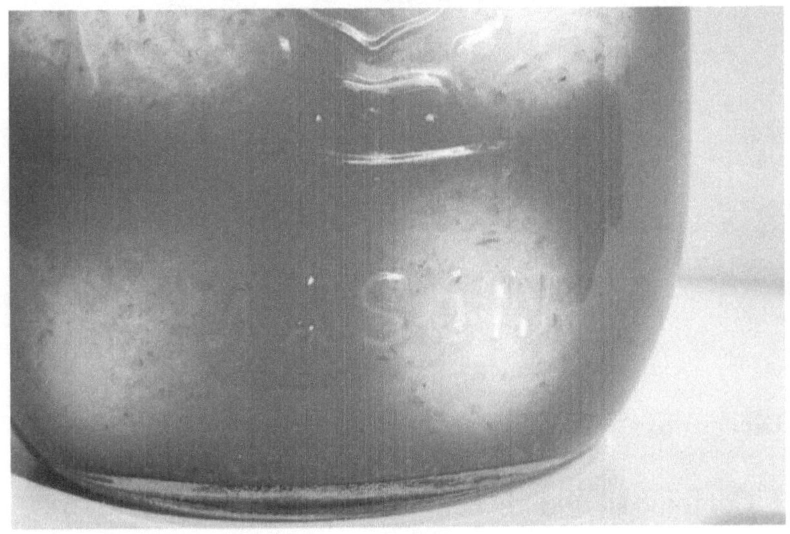

The sriracha flavor will have your mouth-watering in anticipation. The longer you let these eggs marinate the better the taste.

Preparation Time: 10 minutes

Servings: 12

Ingredients:

- 12 ounces white vinegar
- 8 ounces water
- 1 small sliced onion
- 2 ½ ounces sriracha sauce
- 1 teaspoon sea salt
- 12 peeled hard-boiled eggs

Directions:

1. Combine all ingredients except for eggs in a pan and bring mixture to a simmer

2. Remove from heat and let cool for 10 minutes.

3. Put eggs in a 32-ounce jar with a lid. Pour liquid from the pan over the eggs, leaving ¼" of space at the top.

4. Seal jar with the lid and put in the refrigerator for 2-4 days. Shake the jar occasionally.

Quebec Pickled Eggs

When I live in Quebec, these eggs were a daily staple that added taste to every meal. Ii like to eat these with a bit of vinegar drizzled over.

Preparation Time: 15 minutes

Servings: 12

Ingredients:

- 12 peeled hard-boiled eggs
- 2 slices fresh ginger root
- 1 teaspoon black peppercorns
- 12 whole cloves
- 1 bay leaf
- 16 ounces distilled white vinegar
- 4 ounces water
- 1/3 ounce salt

Directions:

1. Wrap cloves, ginger, peppercorns and bay leaf in a cheesecloth loosely

2. Combine vinegar, water and salt in a saucepan. Place cheesecloth in the pan and bring to boil for 10 minutes. Remove cheesecloth and discard contents.

3. Put eggs in a large jar with a lid and pour the hot mixture from the pan over the eggs. Seal with the lid.

4. Chill in the refrigerator for 2-4 days before serving.

Easy Pickled Eggs

This 3-ingredient egg recipe is simple and delicious. Slice these eggs up after they marinate and eat with some fresh bread and cheese.

Preparation Time: 15minutes

Servings: 24

Ingredients:

- 12 peeled hard-boiled eggs
- 15 ounce can pickled beets with juice
- 2 ounces red onion, sliced

Directions:

1. Place eggs in a large jar with a wide mouth and lid. Pour beets, juice and onion into the jar and seal.

2. Chill in the refrigerator for 2-3 days. Shake jar to mix up ingredients occasionally.

Pickled Eggs in Beer

The beer adds an amazing flavor to these hard-boiled eggs that everyone will adore. This recipe is the perfect party dish for the appetizer table.

Preparation Time:15minutes

Servings:24

Ingredients:

- 24 small hard-boiled eggs, peeled
- 12 ounces beer
- 16 ounces vinegar
- ½ ounce pickling spice
- ½ ounce parsley flakes

Directions:

1. Poke holes in the hard-boiled eggs with a fork and place in a large jar with a lid.

2. Combine the rest of the ingredients in a bowl and mix well. Pour mixture over the eggs until completely covered in liquid.

3. Seal jar and place in refrigerator for 3-4 days before serving.

Best Pickled Eggs

The peppercorns and allspice add flavor and depth to these pickled eggs. These eggs take a month to marinate to perfection so while you are waiting for the first batch, start on a second.

Preparation Time: 15minutes

Servings: 12

Ingredients:

- 12 peeled hard-boiled eggs
- 32 ounces distilled white vinegar
- 6 cloves garlic
- ½ ounce whole white peppercorns
- ½ ounce whole allspice
- 2 slices fresh ginger root

Directions:

1. Mix all ingredients except for eggs in a pan and simmer for 10 minutes.

2. Place eggs in a jar with a lid and pour vinegar mixture over top until submerged.

3. Seal jar and immerse in a preserving pan with enough water to cover the jars with 1" of water. Cover the pan and bring to a boil for 10 minutes.

4. Remove jars from water and cool to room temperature.

5. Store in the refrigerator for 30 days before using.

Last Minute Pickled Egg

Try this recipe when you are running short on time and ideas for your next gathering, this last-minute dish tastes delicious after marinating for a few short days.

Preparation Time:15minutes

Servings:12

Ingredients:

- 12 peeled hard-boiled eggs
- 8 ounces tarragon vinegar
- 8 ounces water
- 1 ounce white sugar
- 1/2 teaspoon celery seed
- 1 minced clove garlic
- 1 teaspoon salt
- 2 bay leaves

Directions:

1. Place eggs in a jar with a lid.

2. Mix all ingredients except for eggs in a medium pan and bring to a boil. Reduce heat and simmer for 30 minutes. Remove from heat and cool to room temperature.

3. Pour vinegar mixture over eggs, leaving 1/4" of space at the top. Place in the refrigerator for 2-3 days.

German Pickled Eggs

Pour some oil and vinegar on the pickled eggs before eating for maximum flavor. I like to serve these as an appetizer at parties.

Preparation Time:15 minutes

Servings:12

Ingredients:

- 8 ounces 5% vinegar
- 8 ounces water
- 1 ounce salt
- 10 peeled hard-boiled eggs
- 2 whole bay leaves
- 3 cloves garlic
- 1/2 teaspoon whole peppercorns
- 1/2 teaspoon whole caraway seeds

Directions:

Mix 5% vinegar, water and salt in a stainless-steel bowl until salt is dissolved.

Gather the ingredients.

Add the rest of the ingredients except for the eggs

Place eggs in a large glass jar with a lid. Pour the vinegar mixture over the eggs until submerged, seal and refrigerate for 3-4 days before serving.

Beet Pickled Eggs II

Serve these beets and eggs as a tasty treat with some crusty bread and some sharp cheese. I like to eat these on some bread with mayo and tomato when I want a special snack.

Preparation Time:20 minutes

Servings:12

Ingredients:

- 6 peeled hard-boiled eggs
- 2 peeled beets, cut into ½" cubes
- 16 ounces water
- 8 ounces apple cider vinegar
- 2 ounces granulated sugar
- ½ ounce peppercorns
- 1 teaspoon salt

Directions:

1. Pour 16 ounces of water in a saucepan and simmer beets on medium heat until tender, about 35 minutes.

2. Remove beets from the water with a slotted spoon and set aside in a bowl.

3. Stir in vinegar, sugar, salt and peppercorn until sugar is dissolved.

4. Place eggs and beets in a jar with a lid and pour vinegar mixture in the jar until beets and eggs are submerged. Seal the jar and place in the refrigerator for 3-4 days.

Turmeric Pickled Eggs

The turmeric adds a lovely flavor to these pickled eggs you will love. Slice these eggs up and drizzle with some oil and vinegar before eating.

Preparation Time:20 minutes

Servings:6

Ingredients:

- 6 peeled hard-boiled eggs
- 8 ounces apple cider vinegar
- 4 ounces water
- 1/2 teaspoon turmeric, ground
- 1/3 ounce mustard seeds
- 1 teaspoon salt
- 1 teaspoon granulated sugar

Directions:

1. Pour vinegar and water in a pan and bring to a boil. Add the rest of the ingredients except for the eggs and stir well until sugar dissolves completely.

2. Place eggs in a jar with a lid and pour the brine over the eggs until submerged. Seal and place in the refrigerator for 3-4 days before serving.

Jalapeno Pickled Eggs Recipe

The jalapeno flavor is spicy and addictive in this amazing recipe. I like to serve these eggs with some mustard, cheese and fresh bread.

Preparation Time:20 minutes

Servings:6

Ingredients:

- 6 peeled hard-boiled eggs
- 8 ounces white vinegar
- 4 ounces water
- 3 halved jalapeno peppers, seeds and ribs removed
- 1 small halved onion, sliced thin
- 3 peeled garlic cloves
- 1 ½ ounces granulated sugar
- 1 teaspoon peppercorns
- 1/2 teaspoon mustard seeds

Directions:

1. Pour vinegar and water in a pan and bring to a boil. Add jalapeno, onion, garlic, sugar, mustard and peppercorns to the pan mixture and stir well. Simmer for 5 minutes until sugar has dissolved.

2. Place eggs in a jar with a lid. Remove peppers, onions and garlic from the liquid in the pan with a slotted spoon and place in the jar. Pour the brine from the pan into the jar and seal.

3. Place in the refrigerator for 3-4 days before serving.

Jalapeno Pickled Eggs

This is another spicy recipe for jalapeno pickled eggs that is addictive and unique. The longer these eggs marinate, the spicier and more intense they will taste.

Preparation Time: 20 minutes

Servings: 10

Ingredients:

- 18 peeled hard-boiled eggs
- 16 ounces white vinegar
- 1 small sliced onion
- ¼ ounce mustard seeds
- ¼ ounce dill seeds
- ¼ ounce black pepper
- 6 cloves garlic
- 8 ounces canned whole jalapeno peppers
- 6 drops Frank's hot sauce

Directions:

1. Place eggs in a jar with a lid.

2. Mix the rest of the ingredients in a saucepan and bring to a boil for 15 minutes

3. Pour vinegar mixture into the jar until eggs are submerged. Add hot water if needed.

4. Seal jar and place in the refrigerator for 7-10 days before serving.

Spicy Pickled Eggs II

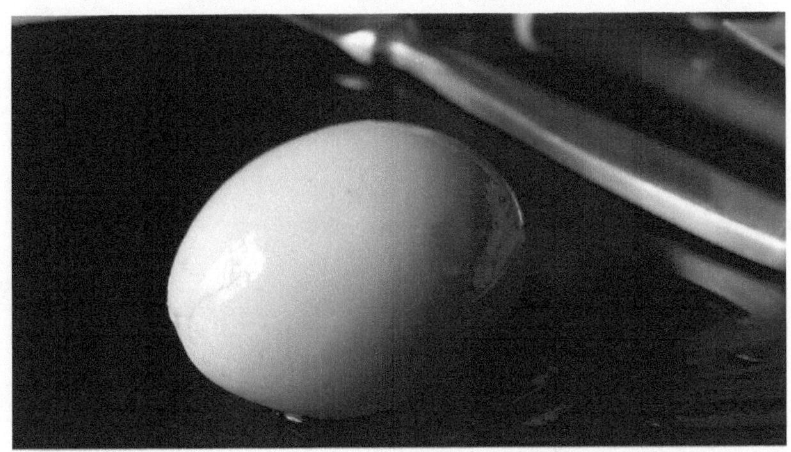

I love the flavour of the brown sugar mixed with sriracha in this simple recipe. These spicy pickled eggs taste amazing sliced or whole with some mayonnaise and a cold beer.

Preparation Time: 20 minutes

Servings: 6

Ingredients:

- 12 peeled hard-boiled eggs
- 18 ounces apple cider vinegar
- 6 ounces red wine vinegar
- ½ ounce kosher salt
- ½ ounce sriracha hot sauce
- 1 ounce brown sugar
- 1 bay leaf
- ½ ounce black peppercorns
- 4 peeled cloves garlic, cut in half

Directions:

Combine all ingredients except for the eggs in a saucepan and bring to a boil. Remove the mixture from heat and chill in the refrigerator.

Place eggs in a jar with a lid and pour the brine into the jar until eggs are submerged.

Seal the jar and place in the refrigerator for 7-10 days.

Habanero And Jalapeno Pickled Eggs

Serve these spicy and tasty treats with some pretzels and an ice-cold beer. I like to marinate these in the brine for 1 month before cracking the jar open and stuffing my face with them!

Ingredients:

- 16 ounces white vinegar
- 4 ounces water
- 4 ounces granulated sugar
- 1 teaspoon salt
- 1 teaspoon pickling spice
- 2/3 ounce red pepper flakes
- 8 whole cloves
- 1 cinnamon stick
- 3 habanero peppers, sliced
- 3 jalapeno peppers, sliced
- 1 red bell pepper, sliced
- 1/4 white onion

Directions:

Mix all ingredients in a pan and bring to a simmer for 15-20 minutes. Stir occasionally.

Place eggs in a jar with a lid and pour the brine from the pan into the jar until eggs are submerged.

Seal the jar and place in the refrigerator for 3 weeks or longer.

Turmeric Pickled Eggs II

This is another recipe for turmeric pickled eggs you will enjoy! I like to mash these eggs up with some mayonnaise and eat them as egg salad sandwich filling.

Preparation Time: 20 minutes

Servings: 6

Ingredients:

- 10 ½ ounces apple cider vinegar
- 4 ounces water
- 1 ounce white sugar
- 1 teaspoon fine grain salt
- 1/3 ounce turmeric, ground
- 1/2 thinly sliced onion
- ½ ounce whole peppercorns
- 6 peeled hard-boiled eggs

Directions:

Combine apple cider vinegar, water, white sugar, salt and turmeric in a saucepan and bring to a simmer until sugar dissolves. Stir often.

Place onion, peppercorns and eggs in a jar with a lid and pour the brine over the eggs until submerged. Seal lid and place in the refrigerator for 10-14 days.

Turmeric-Pickled Deviled Eggs

This recipe uses turmeric to create a delicious flavor you will love. These deviled eggs make a nice potluck item for office parties and social gatherings.

Preparation Time: 20 minutes

Servings: 12

Ingredients:

- 16 ounces water
- 8 ounces apple cider vinegar
- 1 ounce fresh turmeric, grated
- 2 3/8 teaspoons kosher salt, divided
- 12 peeled hard-boiled large eggs
- 3/4 teaspoon Madras curry powder
- 1/4 teaspoon cumin, ground
- 2 ounces canola mayonnaise
- 2 ounces plain 2% Greek yogurt, reduced-fat
- 1 ounce fresh chives, chopped
- Extra chives for garnish

Directions:

Mix water, apple cider vinegar, grated turmeric and 1/3 ounce of kosher salt in a large jar. Add eggs to the mixture in the jar and place in the refrigerator overnight. Shake the jar occasionally to stir the mixture.

Drain eggs from the jar and pat dry.

Heat a small frying pan on medium heat and cook and stir curry powder and cumin in the pan for 1 minute. Remove from heat and let mixture in the frying pan cool.

Slice eggs crosswise and remove yolks. Place yolks in a blender.

Flatten the bottom of the sliced egg halves by slicing a small piece off the bottom. Arrange hollowed-out egg whites on serving dish.

Add mayonnaise, Greek yogurt, curry and the rest of the salt to the blender and process until smooth

Evenly divide filling among the eggs on the platter and garnish with chives before serving.

Conclusion

When you want a snack that is unique and delicious, give one of these 30 recipes a try. All you need is a carton of eggs, a jar and other simple ingredients to create a flavourful appetizer everyone will enjoy. Whether you decide to eat these dishes sliced, deviled or just pop them into your mouth whole, you will never regret waiting for these tasty treats.

Dear Reader,

Thank you very much for choosing my book. I hope you really enjoy it. If don't mind I would like to ask you to leave a review after reading.

Thanks.

Sincerely yours,

Stephanie Sharp

For announcements about new releases, please follow my author page on Amazon.com! (Look for the Follow Bottom under the photo) You can find that at *https://www.amazon.com/author/stephanie-sharp* or Scan QR-code below.